The Caduceus Solution

The Caduceus Solution

The Simple Secret to Lifelong Wellness

By

Elizabeth and Friends

Edited by R. Bruce Lockhart

Acknowledgements

No one really does anything by themselves. So many have contributed to the writing of this book that it would take another book to mention every one of them. We are deeply grateful for the contributions and encouragement of so many and for those that have shown us that our theory works. Their graciousness has brought us lasting, loving changes.

Contents

Introduction

Imagine what it would be like to have *no health concerns at all for the rest of your life.* Most likely, nothing you have learned before would make this seem possible to you. There is a way! These pages are dedicated to setting you on a path of health for the rest of your life. While the approach and method are psychological, the results are physical.

For many years, science has incorporated into medical practice the idea that psychology has a powerful impact on health. This is a remarkable idea! Dr. Dean Ornish, after years of working with heart patients, realized that above all else, a patient's loving relationships with others is the most important factor in aiding their recovery. Other medical professionals, such as Dr. Herbert Benson, author of the Relaxation Response, have discovered that there is a real relationship between cultivating a peaceful mind and physical health.

Our intention is to show you how to shift your focus from a concern with the body's health to the cultivation of a truly happy state of mind. We believe that you can become healthy by letting a true sense of well-being permeate your life. As a result of this process, you will also learn how to communicate more lovingly, and increase your ability to become a good friend.

In these pages we will focus on the powerful concept of the *superconscious*: an aspect of the mind, recognized by the psychiatrist, Dr. Carl Jung. It is the part of the mind from which you can learn to derive truly peaceful and joyous thoughts that affect your health, safety and prosperity.

The brain and the mind are very different entities. The brain is a physical organ that depends upon the mind for all that we learn and experience as consciousness. Our awareness, our understanding, all that we see and experience, and all of our beliefs depend upon what we choose to accept within our minds as truth, whether or not it is true.

We believe that through this book you will begin to realize your destiny as a perfectly healthy and perfectly loving being. We incorporated into these pages examples of others who have experienced healing through the methods that we present here. Their names have been changed to protect their privacy.

You may realize, as you read and accept these ideas, that your past approaches to health were quite different from what is advocated here. Never feel upset about past learning; instead, you can decide to be happy that you are learning healthy new ways *now*.

How to Use this Book

The idea of sickness as a "decision" is likely to be a new idea to you. Many new ideas take time and experience to fully accept. This book will be the beginning of a new understanding that you can integrate into your life. After reading it through the first time, return to it to review the passages that most appeal to you. You can use those passages to prepare your mind for short periods of quiet listening. Let them steer your mind along healthier lines.

You might want to use the book to help formulate questions, and then just listen quietly for an answer. You may want to meditate on a particular sentence and allow related thoughts to come to you. The exercises that we suggest are intended to help you access your superconscious. They should give you a sense of peace and improved health.

Affectual Psychology and the Source of Health

This book is about decision-making. There are certain decisions that you can make about how to best use your mind and body, decisions which will help you to restore and maintain your health. Medicine cannot ultimately provide true, perfect, and lasting health. But please don't interpret our message as a condemnation of medicine, diet, or exercise. While we do not believe that such things can ultimately provide perfect health, we recognize that they can be temporary aids.

We believe there is some unhealthy, unhappy, and unloving decision or false idea in your mind which gives *a purpose* to every illness and that you have the resource to the remedy available to you at all times.

Psychosomatic illnesses, hysterical disease, and hypochondria are examples of the impact the mind can have on health. It is difficult to accept the idea that someone in a state of mental stress would actually "choose" sickness, but it seems to be the case. A person may become ill to relieve psychological stresses. We believe that health can be improved through the elimination of inner conflict and the development of a truly peaceful, truly loving state of mind in which one is freer to make decisions that will result in a healthier state of mind and healthier body.

Our ideas are based on, what we call Affectual Psychology. It is concerned with the mind in terms of its affect on all perceptions. It is about the affect of thought on behavior and the physical. It aims to educate and correct thinking rather than to merely control actions. Affectual Psychology presumes that everyone has a benevolent inner nature and access to the "superconscious mind," the source through which an entirely peaceful, happy, healthy, and constructive self-concept may be developed.

Your Inner Guide to Health

You always have access to the superconscious: a higher part of your mind, that is above consciousness. The superconscious is the source of all thought and emotion that produces tranquility, joy, and loveliness. Just as a jet flies above the earth and through the clouds to where the sun always shines, any thoughts that disturb and prevent inner peace can be driven into the pure clear light of the superconscious. In this light, all dark and threatening thoughts are dispelled or exchanged for peaceful and harmonious ones. This will result in a new, more peaceful perception. It may appear as a new thought or idea; it may change your point of view; it may completely transform your perception. As you learn to access your superconscious more and more, it will gently and peacefully affect you. All of your actions and responses will naturally become more helpful and harmonious.

The superconscious is the home of your Inner Guide and Teacher; everyone has an Inner Guide that can lead one to perfect health. The Inner Guide is not the same thing as "conscience." Conscience can be a useful mechanism; for example, if one feels guilty, it may helpfully indicate that something *is* wrong. However, conscience often promotes guilt and conflict, rather than eliminates it. On the other hand, your Inner Guide is a loving, benevolent force within you that can provide peaceful answers for you, and all concerned, in every situation. Its goal and its gift is your inner peace.

Of what value is inner peace? Inner peace and health go hand in hand. Perfect physical and mental health is the result of peaceful, loving, and forgiving decisions. By training our minds to think and respond in happier, gentler, more appreciative, and more forgiving ways, we can achieve radiant health. When peace enters the heart, joy and health will follow.

There is no perceived problem that cannot be solved when brought to the level of the superconscious. Every unhappy and unloving thought or feeling can be resolved there. All of the dark, hostile, or threatening thoughts that trouble us can be removed. These destructive thoughts are produced by our own agreement with some angry, fearful, or guilty idea that crosses our mind. Without guidance and training, we may be unable to resist reacting negatively.

When these troublesome thoughts, or "mental blocks," are removed, new possibilities suddenly become available to us. In partnership with our Inner Guide, we make a commitment, to discover a peaceful remedy for every conflict. This produces a "new cause," a new motivation, and a new reason. This new reason is independent of the tyranny of guilt, anger or fear. Whenever we choose to seek a peaceful answer to any problem, we are asking for the aid of our Inner Guide.

"It is from your peace of mind that a peaceful perception of the world arises." – *A Course in Miracles*

The Caduceus and the Rod of Asclepius

There are two well-known symbols that aptly illustrate our theory. These two ancient symbols that have been long associated with the medical arts are pictured on the front and back covers of this book: they are the "caduceus" and the "rod of Asclepius." These two symbols are often seen on medicines, healing aids, medical buildings and the name plates of physicians and nurses. Symbols always invite individual interpretation and as we grow in wisdom, some symbols may be seen in more meaningful, universal, ways and others seen as completely meaningless.

These two symbols lend themselves beautifully to the real secret of good health. Our interest is not in the myths associated with these symbols but rather in what is revealed by the symbols themselves. The rod of Asclepius symbolizes the problem of illness and the Caduceus represents the solution to it.

Asclepius was a mythical healer, and the rod of Asclepius is often used to embellish an ambulance. The snake is a traditional symbol of deception (i.e., in the Garden of Eden) and, therefore, for us the image carries a strong implication that illness involves a deception. To us, this ancient figure represents the predicament of the patient. It is a picture of a solitary snake clinging to, and entwined around, a cypress branch. The snake is the patient clinging to "dead" ideas or unhappy thoughts of guilt, anger, fear or hate. The branch has been cut off from the symbolic Tree of Life and is dead. We see this image as a symbol of a sick or injured person who feels vulnerable and alone, separate from others, and cut off from the source of peace, unity, and the true joy of life.

The caduceus is a symbol associated with the mythical Roman god, Mercury. Mercury is the god of communication and good news, and he is usually depicted holding the caduceus. The caduceus suggests that the patient has power over the deception that leads to illness because he is not alone or without help.

The caduceus comprises two snakes perfectly enjoined around a rod with a circle or sphere at the top of it. The heads of the snakes are just below a pair of wings which represent the entrance to the superconscious, the higher sphere of thought beyond the physical. The rod suggests the channel through which the sphere of higher loving thought is communicated to consciousness. The perfect alignment of the wings with the rod, the relaxed union of the two snakes, and the symmetry of the entire figure combine to suggest perfect health, which is nothing more than peace, harmony, and happiness with oneself and with others. The caduceus reveals that the remedy you seek is always available to you through your acceptance of the peaceful and joyous thoughts that emanate from the superconscious.

Communication vs. Attack

It is essential to develop our relationship with our Inner Guide because it is an integral part of who we are. It will help us to make decisions that have a source in the superconscious and to maintain true, loving communication, but we must allow it to have a resting place within our mind. As we accept our Inner Guide, and learn to access it, our understanding of ourselves and our relationships with others will change. We will be guided in how to change our perception of them, and our interactions with them will take on the purpose of mutual happiness.

Communication is the art of cooperating and sharing with others, and is essential to the achievement of happiness. Communication brings joy; it demonstrates, or is expressed or shared in some form that produces happiness. The process of acquiring such a high level of communication depends upon cooperation with your Inner Guide in making decisions about what your purpose with another is, as well as decisions about what needs to be said or done. The goal is always to produce a mutually beneficial outcome. True communication contributes to the happiness of both the giver and the receiver. Forgiveness of yourself and others, expressions of gratitude, and appreciation for others, are especially high forms of communication that well serve the purpose of extending love, peace, and joy.

Underlying many laws, ethics, religious precepts, rules, and good manners is the worthwhile desire to maintain and extend peace within society. A civilized society that can continue to turn more and more towards true peacefulness would only be possible if humans were able to access a higher level of communication. The peace, joy, and health of the entire human race depend upon effective communication with our Inner Guide, whose only purpose is our true happiness.

The opposite of communication is "attack". Real communication does not involve criticism, complaint, or condemnation of others. Criticizing, complaining, and condemning are all forms of attack. If you are currently thinking or expressing yourself in such a way, there is no need to become anxious about it. Do not attack yourself for attacking others! Just try to realize that when the urge to complain, criticize, or condemn arises, it is always better to *think differently*. Learn to recognize every attack on another as a sign of a problem that needs to be resolved. Understand that you attack *because you are not happy,* and that attacking can never make you happy.

It is possible to turn your criticisms, complaints, and grievances over to your Inner Guide and exchange them for a different perception of another or a situation. They may be resolved almost instantly; or your Inner Guide may direct you to someone who can help you resolve them. You will learn to withhold negative responses and to find positive ways to respond that bring peace to yourself and the other. You will learn that if you begin to respond negatively, you can always change course and conclude on a more positive note.

As your dedication to communication and peace increases, you will be able to control and dispel angry thoughts whenever they occur. You can eventually reach a state in which such negative thoughts are immediately and effortlessly dismissed only to be replaced by thoughts that will instantly return you to a happier and peaceful state. True communication produces a gracious attitude, encourages peace, and inspires mutual happiness.

Is it possible for one's thoughts to really attack another person? Certainly our past experience demonstrates that our own negative, destructive thoughts, if left unchecked, can lead to a verbal or physical attack. Yet everyone has the ability to choose how to react to what they hear or see. When a person decides to attack another, it is a learned response, and it is possible to learn to respond differently.

Throughout history, leaders of nations have attempted to manipulate people's thoughts in an attempt to produce in them a predisposition toward hatred and attack upon perceived enemies. Ironically, however, negative thoughts are more apt to hurt oneself than one's intended target because of the state of mind that

11

they produce in the attacker. Where conflict reigns in the heart, joy and health are displaced, and misery follows. History bears this out.

Recall the following schoolyard taunt:

"Sticks and stones may break my bones, but words can never hurt me!"

As with many such pronouncements, the profound truth of this expression is clouded by our long familiarity with it. The saying really illustrates an important distinction between meaning and meaninglessness. It expresses the wise understanding that words that attack have no real power and, thus, need not have an effect. It decrees that each person has the power to decide whether or not to allow words to produce anger, fear, guilt, or injury; whether or not to allow them to have power and meaning. On the other hand, kind, gentle, constructive words, because of their loving, superconscious source, have real power to restore peace of mind and contribute to good health. You cannot be damaged by words of attack when you realize that real security lies in the realm of love.

It is important to learn how to distinguish between meaningfulness and meaninglessness. Most people would not call a hostile argument a "meaningful experience"; however, most would agree that the resolution of a conflict is indeed meaningful. When you recognize the meaninglessness of an attack, it loses its power to affect you. As you learn to distinguish what is meaningful from that which is meaningless, attack thoughts will no longer have a purpose for you.

As you gain experience, you will learn to recognize attack thoughts and how to dispel them. The urge to criticize, complain, or condemn others will be redirected toward a resolution that works for all concerned whenever anything interferes with your peace. You will desire to communicate rather than attack. Your desire to make a friend, rather than an enemy, of someone will increase. You will begin to learn the real meaning and value of communication. You will discover the secret to perfect physical and mental health. How is this possible?

Everyone has some experience of the joy that comes from being in close communication with another. As you learn how to truly and effectively communicate, you will achieve an equilibrium that maintains peace and joy. This improvement in mental health can truly affect your physical well-being. When that is achieved, you will understand that this peaceful, joyous state is the natural state of being, the state in which we were always meant to be

Questioning and Listening

Questioning and listening are essential to developing true communication with anyone. This is also true about communication with your Inner Guide. It is always helpful to consult your Inner Guide whenever you become conflicted about anything.

When seeking peaceful answers, ask questions in a way that does not assign blame to yourself or the other. You or others involved in any conflict may be very mistaken about something, but there is no useful purpose in assigning blame.

When asking questions of your Inner Guide (or of anyone else, for that matter), please be patient. You may need to take the time necessary to think of a useful question and to fully hear and process the answer. For example, when you become angry with someone, you can ask your Inner Guide questions like these, which ask for a meaningful answer:

"Can I see this person and the situation in a more peaceful way?"

"How can I see this person in an innocent light?"

"Do I have all the facts to justify my anger?"

"What does this person really need?"

"Is this person breaking my personal rules?"

14

"What is the purpose of this relationship?"

"Is there something new I can learn from this situation?"

"How would I want someone to react towards me, if the situation were reversed?"

The remarkable thing about this kind of questioning is that it *transforms an impulse to attack or reject into a desire to help and be helped.* The best questions seek another point of view that may provide new information or a different perspective. Always take a moment to calm your mind before asking a question of any person (or of your Inner Guide); then *listen.* Often the first answer you hear will not "work;" it may be something you have thought of before that has never resolved anything. The truest answers do not dwell on the past; they address the present without any negative past reference at all. A good answer will produce a lighter, happier, more secure feeling in everyone involved in the question.

Though you may have difficulty believing it, *your happiness is not dependent on the thoughts, words, or actions of others.* As your mind strengthens in commitment to meaningful communication and as you learn to dismiss the idea that a meaningless attack must affect you, *your body will become healthy in order to serve the new loving cause that has been created by you with the help of your Inner Guide.*

15

Defensiveness

You become defensive when you believe that you are being attacked by what someone says or does; when you are attacking yourself through worrying or holding on to grievances; when you are dwelling on past disappointments, failures or regrets; or when you are fearful about the future. Retaliation, rejection of others, withdrawal, and denial are among the defenses that you employ to justify and protect yourself against a perceived threat to pride, position, or property. This process leads to a vicious cycle that perpetuates negative thoughts and feelings. This happens because any attempt to condemn a perceived attack, to return any attack, or to project anger, fear, and guilt only increases conflict and further disrupts communication and peace of mind.

With the help of your Inner Guide, you can instead use those defenses in a positive way that induces a sastisfactory resolution for you and the other. If you deny anger by deciding that peace, instead of conflict, is your true desire, then a different response should be forthcoming. You may even laugh with delight at an answer you may hear. If you refuse to believe that another's attack can affect you, the urge to attack back should be suddenly redirected towards a peaceful response. If you reject the notion that conflict is useful in any way and ask your Inner Guide to help you to see the situation in a different way, you should be able to withdraw anger from it.

It is entirely within your power to change your view of whomever or whatever seems to be a source of conflict—to see things in a different, kindlier light. Amazingly, this peaceful state of mind will result in improved health.

The Cause of Illness

Sickness has a purpose. It can be viewed as a way of separating ourselves from others, shutting off communication with them, a method of problem solving, or even an attempt to punish another. Sickness can also be a means of self-punishment.

Sickness involves an attack on the body. All attack is a defensive response to some idea of fear, guilt or anger that is unresolved in your mind. The onset of illness may be an indication of a guilty judgment of yourself or another; or it may be the fear of some dark, looming threat in the mind; or it may come from the awareness of a mistake that you think requires punishment of yourself or another. But who makes decisions, passes judgments, feels threatened, and assigns blame? Who initiates the attack that activates the "defense mechanism" of sickness? Could it be you?

The belief that sickness comes from the mind is often misinterpreted as an *accusation* that the sick person is "faking" illness or as an insinuation that they somehow deserve to be sick. For this reason, many are not comfortable with the idea of sickness as a defense mechanism. The idea that a patient's diagnosis with an illness—the common cold, schizophrenia, cancer, mental disabilities, and the numerous conditions that are considered chronic or congenital —can be in any way a matter of personal choice may seem unfair and unreasonable to you. If you are dealing with an illness as you read this, the idea that you might be somehow "responsible" for it may even make you feel angry or guilty. This is because of the false association between responsibility and guilt.

We do not believe a person should be "blamed" for becoming ill. Blame is a meaningless and useless concept. We take great joy in the positive understanding that we are responsible for our health and that we have within us everything necessary to become perfectly healthy and even affect another's health.

To some it may seem that the most reasonable argument against this line of thinking lies in the case of newborn babies who are diagnosed with an illness. It may seem reasonable to think that they could not possibly have yet chosen sickness for themselves, but we believe that every human being is born with a set of ideas. It is in how they are nurtured when they are in this condition that will contribute most to their recovery. Fortunately, almost anyone finds it very easy to accept a baby's lovingness; a perception of them that is a major step towards assisting them to achieve a healthy state.

To truly heal, the mind must be recognized as the decision maker. It is really the mind that needs healing. When you make the decision that it is safe to be well and happy, what is needed for healing will occur. Even a moment spent in peace and quiet can result in healing. That is because, in such a state, you are accessing the superconscious and accepting its effects. It nurtures the mind and affects the body.

With this realization we can influence and help others to be well. However, each person has the power to make their own decisions, and no one should ever feel guilty or angry if someone becomes ill.

***

Vivian got an urgent call from her close friend, Natalie, who was distressed that her granddaughter had just been born prematurely and diagnosed with a severe illness. After the phone call, Vivian used a healing exercise that is included in the book. She felt completely confident that the new baby, Amy, would heal and hoped for the best result. The baby completely recovered within a few months. When Amy was almost two years old, Vivian was visiting with her. They were playing an old fashioned game of patty cakes. Vivian had cut her thumb while gardening and it was mending well. The little child noticed it while they were playing and took Vivian's hand to have a good look at her thumb. She gave it a dispassionate look, then gently kissed it, and let go of Vivian's hand with no concern at all. Vivian was delighted at the child's perfect demonstration of how to help another heal. If you see a need for healing, offer love and let go.

Encouraging Healthiness

When a child is not feeling well, a wise parent may recommend that they take some rest. Quiet rest is widely believed to be restorative. People have long realized that rest is helpful to recovery from illness. We believe that this is true to a greater extent than most people imagine. It is not really the body that needs rest. It is the development of a restful and peaceful mind that is most critical to keeping the body strong.

As we have said, there is a sense in which traditional medicine recognizes sickness as a psychological defense: i.e., in cases of psychosomatic illness, hypochondria, and hysterical illness. What has not been widely recognized is that, unless one allows the ideas behind fears to dissolve, one may be compelled to actually *choose* sickness as the solution to a dilemma. But, in reality, fear, guilt and anger do not cause illness. The belief that they can do so can cause people to accept sickness as inevitable.

Conflicts within the mind do not have to affect you physically and, when a conflict is resolved and illness is no longer useful to you, health can be restored. The acceptance of this idea is essential to one's inner peace.

Every parent is aware of at least one common manifestation of illness as a psychological process. Our children become "sick" from fear of retribution when

21

they have not done tomorrow's homework, when they are afraid to face a bully at school, when they fear being separated from loved ones, or due to some other anxiety. Children who seek to escape school through illness may decide on their own that it is safe to be well again, once they are no longer disturbed by the consequences of going to school. They may spontaneously and naturally access their Inner Guide, realizing that the threat represented by returning to school is meaningless.

Parents employ a form of natural healing, gently calming, reassuring, and dispelling fears when they realize that what is bothering their child is meaningless. The parent's intervention helps the child to decide that it is safe to rejoin the world and recover. If the fear, anger, guilt, or dark thought that precipitates the need to stay home is dispelled, the child may never use sickness as a defense again! Whether a child is actually manifesting physical symptoms or is simply pretending to be ill to avoid some stress at school, the mechanism for healing is the same. We believe that the type of healing employed by parents in this example—the elimination of unnecessary fear and the application of love—indicates the direction in which all true physical and psychological healing must and will proceed.

In such cases it seems clear, reasonable and hardly controversial to say that psychological defense is at least one *purpose of sickness*. We believe that the understanding of illness as a psychological response is the first step in true healing. When you realize the true cause of sickness and understand its purpose as a "defense mechanism" against a peaceful and loving possibility, it becomes useless and can be discarded. Once you learn to resolve what frightens you, your defenses will no longer have a purpose. As in the case of a child "playing sick" to stay home from school, when your desire to join back in with life recovers, so will your health. When you begin listening calmly and return to communication with your Inner Guide and with others, your health will become radiant again. This is not to say that sick people are "faking it." What we are really saying is that every person who experiences illness needs help with their ideas to restore a peaceful state of mind. The process of recovery is the same in all cases.

***

Caitlin was a normal, happy and healthy girl despite the fact she was a very finicky eater. As her seventh birthday approached, Caitlin was told by her parents that she was going to be a big girl soon, and she would have to begin eating more "healthy" foods. On her birthday, Caitlin's grandmother visited and was surprised that the little girl felt feverish and complained that she did not feel well. Since Catlin had almost never been ill in her entire short life, it occurred to her grandmother that the little girl might be afraid of something. They had a conversation in which Caitlin revealed that she was fearful of being forced to eat different foods. Grandmother spoke with Caitlin's parents. She told them about their daughter's anxiety and pointed out that Caitlin's weight and health were well within the range considered healthy. They agreed to allay the little girls concern and to introduce new foods more slowly. Caitlin recovered her health within hours. Several years later she is still physically healthy and her weight is still considered to be in a healthy range for her height.

***

Eventually you will discover that every fearful, guilty or angry thought or idea is unjustifiable and can be dispelled or exchanged for a peaceful one. Threatening, unpleasant, and destructive people or situations can be seen otherwise and transformed. Dark and negative thoughts do not have to be taken out on the body. To fully achieve a real understanding of this takes time and practice.

Some Thoughts about Food and Drink

As long as you have a body, you will need to eat. Peaceful eating is healthy eating. As the mind becomes more and more oriented towards peaceful thinking, and as the desire to communicate rather than attack increases, your equilibrium will be such that food and drink will be easily digested and what is not necessary for the body's health will be eliminated.

Who decides if what you eat is healthy for your body or will threaten your health? Historically, the nutritional status and perceived danger of certain categories of foods, drinks, chemicals and additives has often changed. This lack of consistency suggests that the sources of such nutritional information may not be reliable. Beliefs can change and it is always important to consider the source of your beliefs and those of others.

We would like to help you develop a peaceful mind in reference to food and drink. One rule that works well is not to deprive your body of food. To deprive or fight yourself is a form of self-attack and this is obviously not conducive to a peaceful state of mind.

Those who feel deprived often exhibit negative emotions such as anger, jealousy and weariness. An upset and worried state of mind can adversely affect one's appetite. Usually those in a calmer state of mind about food and themselves will eat just enough and stop when they are satisfied. Appetites will regulate as your personal cares and concerns are given to your Inner Guide for resolution. Those who are happily engaged in the business of living usually do not overeat, nor do they starve themselves, unless some worrisome or fearful belief is affecting them.

You can use your Inner Guide to help you decide what to eat or for another way to see the food you eat. You may find that you will eat more, or less, at different times and stay quite satisfied either way. It is liberating and healthy to stop worrying about everything you eat. It is healthy to enjoy your food.

Try to become more appreciative and less analytical about your meals. This will bring peace to you. One healthy habit worth developing is to express gratitude for the food you are eating. You can even feel and express appreciation for the cook, the grocery store, the manufacturers and the farmers. That will make for an enjoyable meal! A grateful state of mind will aid in digestion.

In other words, the cultivation of a peaceful, happy and appreciative state of mind is one of the healthiest decisions you can make. If you are someone who has always been strict about your diet, your Inner Guide may have you stay with your program for now. A peaceful and appreciative mind is its first concern.

***

Paul Roberts was an accountant who lived a long, productive life. He was a kind man whose main concern in life was the well-being of his family and friends. He rarely worried about his health and was physically healthy most of his life. His weight was always in what is considered a healthy range. He never thought about his diet. He was unconcerned with the nutritional thinking of the day. His habit was to have three meals a day that consisted of almost any foods. He would drink a variety of beverages, including a moderate amount of alcoholic drinks. He always said grace, setting his mind in a gracious state, before meals. He always enjoyed his meals, commenting on how delicious they were, and he was always appreciative to the cook. We believe that the non-analytical approach to diet exemplified by Paul Roberts can serve as a model for everyone.

***

Forgiveness and Health

As an aspect of communication, forgiveness can become your best defense against illness. How can true forgiveness be used as a defense against sickness? It will become the means that you will employ against some perceived threat instead of deciding to withdraw and become ill. It will keep your mind disposed towards happiness. Those that you fear you've hurt in the past, those that you believe have hurt you or will hurt you in the future, can all be brought into the realm of forgiveness and will affect all.

The decision for pardon, instead of retribution, will automatically establish communication with your Inner Guide. When you are willing to take a moment to reestablish a peaceful, happy state of mind free of guilt and its consequences and to reconsider the conflicting and unloving thoughts that you are holding onto, your Inner Guide will accept your request. Your fearful perception of others and yourself will be exchanged for an answer that will give you peace.

The process of forgiveness begins *now,* in this very moment, to reestablish peace of mind *now.* It overlooks the past and the future. It opens the way for a new answer, a new possibility, and a different future. A mind that accepts the remedy of forgiveness will not continue to dwell on their past mistakes or on those of others. It will not remain disturbed, and it will not continue to believe in retribution. It believes in reparation, but it is not concerned about the *form of reparation;* rather, it trusts that it can be accomplished in a peaceful way with *no loss to anyone.* Forgiveness can only bring gain to all.

The forgiving mind allows error to be *gently* corrected. It recognizes that, although you are responsible for your mistakes, you are not *solely* responsible for their correction, and you need not suffer painful retribution. Forgiveness sets the mind at rest and allows healing to, simply, *be.* Those who have accepted this usually do not repeat their mistakes. They simply outgrow their use for them.

Forgiveness inspires a hopeful state of mind that provides the grounds for healing the mind and affecting the body. At first this is taken on faith, but the results will strengthen your determination, and the goal of developing a forgiving mind will become increasingly desirable.

Forgiveness and Communication

Forgiveness establishes a real basis for communication and affects health. Conversely, condemnation is the basis of all attack and could lead to illness. Most would admit that it is difficult to feel joyously toward those who they believe have hurt them or to whom they harbor grievances.

When you learn how to truly and readily forgive, you will discover the most powerful method of restoring and maintaining perfect, radiant health. Forgiveness restores peace, allows healing, and never makes demands of others in its remedies. It establishes a safe and immediately hospitable environment that invites real solutions. When one feels safe, communication can only improve. It can only help and heal.

Because the idea of true forgiveness originates in the endless resource of the superconscious mind, it is available for your use at all times. Forgiveness has many uses, and one important one, as we stated earlier, is to open the way to emotional, psychological and physical health. You often hear the victims (or the relatives of victims) of violent crime say that they find it necessary to forgive the perpetrator because hatred is "killing" them or "eating away" at them. We believe that this is true and that it should be applied to our everyday lives.

Forgiving others is a way of freeing not only another, but also yourself, from the anger and the guilt you are harboring towards them, which is blocking your peace of mind. The decision to forgive will affect your thoughts and actions, which will become more constructive. The need for your psychological defenses will diminish. The desire to do anything that exacerbates anger and guilt will seem to you a waste of time. The need for vengeance will give way to the desire to accomplish that which benefits others and yourself.

True forgiveness is a means to undo all consequences of the past and all implications for the future. It assures that your own mistakes and those of others are corrected inside and out! Forgiveness can undo the effects of grievances, hurts, and past neglects, or of any other dark thoughts that may occupy your mind. It calls for an enlightened experience of happiness and joy, without retribution or cost to you or another. It allows for a new beginning. We make a distinction between this true forgiveness and the false forgiveness that pardons sometimes but still remembers past offenses, continues to assign blame, and insists on retribution and punishment.

No matter whom or what you are upset about, your own Inner Guide and Teacher is always available to help you. As you turn over your problems and concerns to it, you will experience the love and healing, the harmony and peace that have been hiding in plain sight. Communication will be once again open.

The Beneficence of Forgiveness

Many have been taught and conditioned to believe that they are guilty, at least in some ways, and that there is a stiff price to pay for every infraction against conscience. The saying "As you sow, so shall you reap", really means what you consider worth cultivating, you will cultivate in yourself and not as a statement in any way justifying punishment or retribution.

Whenever we make an accusation against another, whenever we demand punishment, we are acknowledging an underlying belief that to be human is to be guilty. Therefore, every accuser is really a self-accuser. This is why, to forgive others, it is necessary, first of all, to forgive one's self. We all have the responsibility to forgive ourselves. In a sense, it is our only responsibility.

When you accept forgiveness for yourself, you become kind; the necessity for anger, cruelty, vengeance, and retribution disappears completely. You no longer believe that cosmic forces are pitted against you. A self-forgiven person is honest and gentle, confident and courageous (which literally means "heart-centered"). A self-forgiven person is more tolerant of others, and is likely to forgive them no matter what they say or do. A person who is free of the falseness of guilt and the meaninglessness of retribution is free from fear, seeing the truth more clearly and able to properly respond to that which is untrue.

For the self-forgiven person, there is no need to fear attack, or to attack another, nor is there any longer a purpose for illness. When you banish conflict from the heart, you become free from the anxiety, turmoil, and paralysis that it has imposed upon you. You develop the ability to easily discern what is valuable and what is worthless, what is meaningful and what is meaningless, and what matters and what doesn't matter at all. A self-forgiven person is generous and will not use others to achieve selfish goals. Nor do they take on selfless goals that demand loss, because he or she knows that all worthwhile goals benefit everyone and every situation including them. A self-forgiven person is aware that the means to dispel conflict in any and every situation are available to them. Although they may not be sure of the form of the answer, they trust that they will be answered in a peaceful way. A feeling of safety emanates from the forgiven mind, and this feeling is extended to others.

To forgive yourself means to *allow* all your mistakes from the past to be corrected with the help of your Inner Guide. It also means that future mistakes will be corrected. When we choose to forgive rather than condemn, we recognize that we are always deserving of love and healing. No longer will we believe punishment is our just due. As we allow our guilty judgments of ourselves and others to go, we will experience joy and we will experience healing.

In a forgiven state, your memory will keep only the loving thoughts of the past, those you communicated to others and those that others have communicated to you. Everything else is forgotten because it no longer matters. This is the real meaning of living in the present. It is a gift indeed!

Healthy Exercises

The following exercises will help you in accessing the superconscious level of your mind. In conjunction with your Inner Guide you can exchange any form of anger, guilt and fear towards others for a peaceful perception of them. They will help you make new decisions about your relationships that will result in better health. It is recommended that you start with specific problems and people that currently engage you at work, at leisure, and among your family and friends.

An Exercise in Gratitude

This is a simple, easy and straightforward exercise. It can be done anytime and usually brings immediate results. We believe that it will help bring out your natural graciousness and that you will experience happiness and a more peaceful attitude.

Get into a comfortable sitting position in a place where you can be quiet for a few moments. Even one minute of inner focus on what you are grateful for will help.

Take as much time as you like; if you find your mind wandering off the subject, open your eyes and begin again. If you continue to have difficulty focusing, postpone the exercise for a while.

When you are relaxed and focused, simply tell yourself, "I am grateful for [*name specific things*]." Consciously search your thoughts for a minute or two and then relax. In this meditative state, other thoughts that inspire gratitude may occur to you. When you are finished, silently express thanks for the things that occurred to you.

This can be an especially good exercise before going to sleep at night. Try to remember as many beneficial things that occurred during the day, however small they may seem, for which you can feel grateful. It would be especially useful to concentrate on any kind, helpful or happy encounters that you have had with others. You may be surprised by the number of opportunities for gratitude that will occur to you.

This exercise has the additional benefit of setting your mind in a restful state for sleep.

"True gratitude is so close to real love that peace and joy easily follow; they will flow across the mind and extend outward."—*Anonymous*

An Exercise in Forgiveness

This is an exercise adapted from "A Course in Miracles," that will assist you in joining your mind with your Inner Guide to help solve any specific problem that appears to be confronting you:

- Choose a time and place that is as quiet as possible. Get yourself into a comfortable sitting position and relax for a minute.
- Shut your eyes and think to yourself, "My negative thoughts are blocking the benefits that a peaceful mind would show me."
- Pause a moment. You should be feeling comfortable when you proceed. (If at any time you find yourself becoming irritated, or if your mind begins wandering during any point in the exercise, open your eyes and begin again. If the difficulty continues, consider postponing the exercise until another time.)
- Search your mind for any persons or situations that seem to be causing you to feel anger, regret, sadness, anxiety, or any form of negative emotion. Four or five examples are enough for one session. Try to treat them all alike, as best you can. Only a few minutes should be spent in this kind of mind searching. *Be as specific as possible about whom or what these emotions are associated with.*

- Think about each specific person or situation in your mind and identify the specific emotion associated with it. Think to yourself, for example:

  "I am worried about [*something specific*] and am afraid _____ may happen.

  I am angry at [*a specific person*] _____and am afraid _____ may happen.

  I am sad about [*name the specific emotion, person, or circumstance*] and afraid that _____may happen."

After you have uncovered each one of these negative possibilities, say to yourself, "That thought is an attack on myself."

At the end of your session, say to yourself, "I choose to exchange these attack thoughts for a peaceful perception of these persons and situations."

You should feel some sense of relief. Sit quietly for a few moments. Productive thoughts or ideas that help you decide what to do next may occur to you. Often you need do nothing but resume normal activities. Through this exercise, practiced with faith and patience, the answers to your problems will gently unfold.

Eventually the state of mind induced by this process will become a permanent feature of your being.

You can use this exercise from time to time to give up any angry, guilty, or fearful thoughts you may be holding onto. Your darkest secrets and misapprehensions will be safely given up or corrected. Those who have experienced the results of allowing their fears to be corrected find their lives greatly improved; they "function" better in every area of their lives, and they naturally extend forgiveness and, thus, happiness to others.

No matter how long you have held onto grievances about yourself or others, as long as you have some willingness to set these negative thoughts and emotions aside, they can all be dispelled without any guilt, retribution, or punishment. This is a process, and the ideas in these pages can be considered and tried for as long as it takes to achieve the results you desire. Be patient and be kind to yourself if you don't immediately experience joy and peace. Be secure in the knowledge that you have set yourself on the path of healing and will reach the goal of perfect health, which is perfect peace and happiness.

You will become more open to the possibility that you can be happier when you *allow your mind to change.* All of the positive results you seek will be forthcoming. You will become eager to *decide* to change the way you view, react, and respond to every person and situation. You will gain confidence in the process of working with your Inner Guide and communicating with others in a way that produces joy.

***

Janice had four children and a negative view of herself as a mother. She often felt overwhelmed, burdened and inadequate to take care of her children, and she often berated herself. She was diagnosed with a terminal form of cancer and told to make arrangements for imminent death. As she prepared to face this crisis, Janice determined to become more peaceful and happy with herself and those around her. After much self-examination, she began to suspect that her feelings of guilt and her poor self-image were contributing to a physical decline. In spite of the "hopeless" prognosis issued by her physicians, she continued to seek a medical solution, but mainly relied on accessing her superconscious through prayer and quiet meditation with her Inner Guide. Many years later, she is happily living in a seaside community with her children.

***

An Exercise for Health and Well-Being

This is an exercise adapted from "A Course in Miracles." It will assist you in joining with your Inner Guide if you are emotionally upset or experiencing unhealthy physical symptoms:

- Get your body in a comfortable upright position. Sitting up in a chair would work well. Take a moment to calm your mind.
- Tell yourself, "I must have made a wrong decision because I do not like the way I feel. I'm willing to reconsider this decision and decide otherwise." Search your mind for a minute or two and see if you can remember what threatened you. If you are willing to reconsider it, the effects of your decision can be undone with the aid of your Inner Guide. Tell yourself, "I will not keep this decision and will let this decision be undone for me. I am determined to be happier and healthy and allow a peaceful answer to come to me."
- Wait quietly for a few moments. It is entirely possible for you to feel completely free from your past decision.
- If you cannot remember any decision that you made that might lead to upset or illness, you can still listen for guidance. A resolution that you have not thought of before may occur to you.

You may be given another way to see yourself or another. You may be guided to say something to someone that can help you restore your peace of mind.

- You will always be guided in the most peaceful way for you to restore your health. There may be times when seeing a doctor is a part of your solution.

Try to take a few minutes after this exercise and allow your mind to become rested and peaceful before resuming your activities.

During the day, preferably once an hour or more, think to yourself, "For today, I will let my grievances go and let the happiest of answers come to me."

This is a wonderful prescription! You can also use other words that resonate with you and that reflect the idea of letting go of dark thoughts and allowing new and happier ones to come to you.

Many people find that symptoms disappear quite rapidly when they make a firm decision to be well, free of conflict, and physically healthy.

***

William was in his late 60's when his legs began to fail him. Although, many around him believed that a physical decline due to age was inevitable, William did

43

not share that belief. He was familiar with the ideas we have introduced here. He believed in the loving power available to him through the superconscious mind, and he made the decision to be well and live a loving life. Rather than look for a cause for his malady, he decided, as soon as he was having trouble, to join in with his Inner Guide and accept a new cause. William was very fortunate to have an open-minded physician who did not set narrow limits upon the search for true healing. The only non-psychological means of healing that William chose to seek during this period were physical therapy and chiropractic. Over the course of a few months, to the delight and amazement of his friends and family, he completely recovered the full use of his legs.

***

An Exercise for Aiding Others in Health and Well-Being

Take a few moments by yourself, calm your mind, and then welcome your Inner Guide into your thoughts. Think to yourself, "I am determined to see [*name a specific person*] differently. I will not accept them as sick and helpless. Let their past unloving thoughts about themselves all be dissolved and let the peaceful and loving thoughts they need to heal come to them."

Only do the exercise one time for this person and try to perform it with full faith and trust. Your hope and expectation that the best answer will come to them is the most helpful thought to keep with you.

Afterwards, you may want to ask of your Inner Guide, "Can I do anything else for this person?" The form of the answer can vary, but it will always be something that alleviates fear in you and the other person. If this is a friend or relative, your Inner Guide may advise you to establish contact with this person in some way. Such communication can help ease the sense of separation and aloneness that he or she may feel. People can heal more quickly when they sense that someone truly cares for them.

One question that should be considered carefully is "Should I share, with anyone, the information that _____ is ill?" What purpose does it serve?

Science has begun to accept that positive, loving thought and action can contribute significantly to healing. If you want to visit someone feeling ill, it is best to approach them with a hopeful attitude, regardless of the prognosis. The more you trust in healing, the better you are able to help. Don't encourage them to talk about their illness. Your Inner Guide is always with you; try to listen to its suggestions about what to do or say. For example, you might tell them of someone else you know who recovered from what they are experiencing. You might remind them of a kind thing they did for you. You may be able to dispel the dark thoughts they are harboring. Your peaceful presence will help!

You may choose to do this exercise for someone you have not met, in which case nothing but your trust in the influence of the superconscious mind is required.

**

Our friend Tony suffered from migraine headaches for many years. When he was approached with ideas that are contained in these pages, he was unwilling to accept the thought that he could decide for himself to remain pain- free and healthy. One of our authors engaged Tony in a "silent healing" process. She fully expected him to become well and treated him as though he were healed. Since then, he has not suffered from a single migraine.

A Final Testimony

For years, Veronica, accepted various physical symptoms, such as low stamina, chronic indigestion, blotchy skin and tired feet, as just the way she was. She was often conflicted about conditions at her job, especially her relations with her supervisor. One day her sadness and frustration with her predicament became so emotionally overwhelming that, almost without knowing what she was doing, she began fervently asking her Inner Guide for help. She made the decision that she no longer wanted this conflict and determined to do whatever she could to achieve happiness and well-being.

She began to meditate using a technique that she learned from a book called "The Relaxation Response," and she noticed immediate improvement in her state of mind. A short time later one of her friends told her about a book entitled "A Course in Miracles" which very much appealed to her. Within a few months, her anger and resentment toward her job abated.

She developed a new understanding and appreciation of the boss she once despised. She became adept at quickly resolving every conflict on the job and in her personal life by bringing them to the light of the superconscious through the help of her Inner Guide. Friends and co-workers marveled at the improvements in her health and disposition. When she eventually left her job, she did so on friendly terms and still considers her ex-manager a good friend.

What You Are

A forgiven mind is the condition that opens up the way for remembering something else in your unconscious: *your true self*. It unlocks more constructive and creative abilities. Your learning can lead to such heights that *sickness will become impossible for you*. Does this mean your body will never die? At the end of your life journey, the body can be cast off with gratitude for its use to you. This is beyond the focus of our thesis, but it is safe to say there is still more for you to learn about gently returning to your loving origin.

What you are, in Truth, is a loving being. What does that mean? That is a most worthwhile question, but the answer is not a matter of mere words. It is revealed through experience and changes in perception. It lies in happier, more peaceful, more loving thoughts and actions. It leads to radiant mental and physical health.

The self-concept that you hold of yourself now does not completely reflect a loved and loving self. You may even have doubts that a concept of yourself as a wholly loving being could possibly be true. Although your past may support your doubts, the future can prove them to be invalid. You can develop a concept of self that is safe, healthy, loving, and fulfilled in a seemingly insecure and turbulent world. This is also true for all those around you, though they may not appear to you to be healthy or loving now. The example of your forgiveness and love will support them in their own search for happiness and health. It is the purpose of the Inner Guide to help you make such realizations.

There are many methods for joining in and developing a deep, joyful relationship with your Inner Guide, Healer and Teacher. It isn't interested in blaming you for your errors. It only desires to show you the correction of your erroneous ideas, the "ways of your errors," as opposed to the "error of your ways." It wants to help you make decisions that enable you to think and act in a way that will assist you in remembering and manifesting your own loving self.

Understanding that forgiveness of yourself and others is your best defense against illness, accepting the knowledge that your mind is the decision maker in how the body is used, and realizing that you have a loving Inner Guide that will teach and guide you: these are the "secrets" of true health. As you develop an effective healing practice, not only will you be physically healthy, but all of your relationships and experiences will become more loving and lovelier. As Thomas Carlyle wrote, "A loving heart is the beginning of all knowledge."

A Final Thought: Our Desire for You

There has been much confusion through the ages about the source of health and healing. There has also been much confusion about the illusion and reality of love. Sexuality especially needs a close look. It can be used lovingly but often is not. The desire behind that impulse can be redirected in truly loving ways.

We assure you that, with the help of your Inner Guide and others to whom you will be guided, you will learn to discern the difference between what really makes you happy, loving and joyous and what does not. You will eventually learn to laugh at your follies and let love happen.

We leave these pages in your hands with hope and trust that, in communication with your Inner Guide, you will have happier relationships and perfect health.

"Love reverses physical laws."—*Anonymous*

Bibliography

A Course in Miracles is the most advanced and comprehensive work on the thought and methods covered in the preceding pages. Those that are ready for its unconventional teachings on life, health, and human destiny will find it appealing. The text is written in both psychological and spiritual terms. It includes a year's worth of workbook lessons to assist you in training your mind to respond to every circumstance with love, forgiveness, and gratitude.

There are a few versions of the book available for purchase. There are also books written by Doug Thompson on the "Urtext of *A Course in Miracles*" and free copies of the Urtext are available online. It is the original version, before it was published, and contains additional material not included in *A Course in Miracles*.

The following books are also quite beneficial. We do not entirely embrace all of the ideas suggested by them; however, they illustrate and support the theory that decisions of the mind affect the body's health. They also recognize the role of the superconscious in the realization of true health.

How to Stop Worrying and Start Living, by Dale Carnegie. 1948. Simon and Schuster.
This contains numerous accounts of the impact of

mental state on health. It is available in paperback as a Pocket Books edition.

How to Win Friends and Influence People, by Dale Carnegie, 1936. Simon and Schuster.
Examples in this book include demonstrations of the purpose of sickness and the power of deciding to be healthy and happy.

Hidden Power for Human Problems, by Frederick Bailes. 1957. The author overcame a fatal diagnosis. The book includes useful approaches for accessing the superconscious.

The Relaxation Response, by Dr. Herbert Benson and Miriam Klipper. 1985. Penguin Group.
The authors discover and share the health benefits of accessing the peace of the superconscious. This is a highly intelligible guide to the process of meditation. It is very valuable for anyone who wants to more deeply explore the practice of meditation. But please be careful! Beginning practitioners who fail to relinquish angry, guilty, or fearful thoughts may find that their imagination misapprehends unsuppressed thoughts from the superconscious and they may find new things to be angry or fearful about that can lead them into undesirable mental or emotional states. Gentle is the way!

Macbeth, by William Shakespeare.

This great play provides a negative example: a glimpse into the world of a man and woman who fail to access the power and love of the Inner Guide. The scene with Lady Macbeth and her physician is especially compelling in relation to the idea of guilt and psychosomatic illness.